FIRST RESPONDERS
ON 9/11

AMY C. REA

childsworld.com

ABOUT THE AUTHOR

Amy C. Rea grew up in northern Minnesota and now lives in a Minneapolis suburb with her family. She writes frequently about traveling around Minnesota and loves spending time with her family and her silly dog.

Published by The Child's World®
800-599-READ • www.childsworld.com

Copyright © 2025 by The Child's World®
All rights reserved. No part of this book may be reproduced or utilized in any form or by any means without written permission from the publisher.

Photography Credits
Photographs ©: Shawn Baldwin/AP Images, cover, 1; iStockphoto, 5, 16; David Bookstaver/AP Images, 6; National Oceanic and Atmospheric Administration/Library of Congress, 8; Carol M. Highsmith/Library of Congress, 9; Library of Congress, 11; Stephen Chernin/AP Images, 12; Jose Jimenez/Primera Hora/Getty Images News/Getty Images, 15; Leonard Zhukovsky/Shutterstock Images, 18; Anthony Correia/Shutterstock Images, 21; ZTA/ZOB/Z. Tomaszewski/WENN/Newscom, 22; Stuart Nimmo/CP/AP Images, 24; Shutterstock Images, 27 (left); Inna Kharlamova/Shutterstock Images, 27 (middle); Sergii Tverdokhlibov/Shutterstock Images, 27 (right); Daniel Hulshizer/AP Images, 28

ISBN Information
9781503889095 (Reinforced Library Binding)
9781503890862 (Portable Document Format)
9781503892101 (Online Multi-user eBook)
9781503893344 (Electronic Publication)

LCCN 2023950249

Printed in the United States of America

CONTENTS

FAST FACTS 4

CHAPTER ONE
BRENDA BERKMAN 6

CHAPTER TWO
YAMEL MERINO 13

CHAPTER THREE
WILLIAM JIMENO 18

CHAPTER FOUR
**SCOTT STRAUSS AND
PADDY MCGEE 25**

THINK ABOUT IT 29
GLOSSARY 30
SELECTED BIBLIOGRAPHY 31
FIND OUT MORE 31
INDEX 32

FAST FACTS

- On September 11, 2001, **terrorists** flew airplanes into the Twin Towers of the World Trade Center in New York City. They flew another airplane into the Pentagon in Washington, DC. A fourth plane crashed in a field in Pennsylvania.

- The first attack was on the North Tower. The South Tower was hit next. The South Tower collapsed first. The North Tower collapsed about 30 minutes later.

- Brenda Berkman was a firefighter in New York City on 9/11. She was sent to help rescue survivors at the World Trade Center.

- Yamel Merino provided medical care to people being **evacuated** from the World Trade Center.

- William Jimeno was a police officer working at the World Trade Center on 9/11. He and another officer were buried under 20 to 30 feet (6.1 to 9.1 m) of rubble. They were rescued by Scott Strauss and Paddy McGee.

- About 2,750 people died in the World Trade Center attacks, including more than 400 police officers and firefighters.

A memorial in New York City honors first responders who died in the September 11 attacks.

CHAPTER ONE

BRENDA BERKMAN

On September 11, 2001, New York firefighter Brenda Berkman was off duty. She planned to spend her time off working on local elections that day. Then her partner's mother called to ask if they were all right. The mother had seen a plane crashing into the World Trade Center on the news.

◄ **Brenda Berkman (front row, left) joined the New York City Fire Department in 1982. She was part of the city's first class of female firefighters (pictured).**

Berkman thought that the fire department would want her to come to work. "If planes have hit the World Trade Center, they're going to need extra people," she thought. She needed to go to the fire department's headquarters to learn more.

Public transit was no longer running on its usual schedule. Berkman ran toward headquarters. As she hurried down the sidewalk, she went past the fire station where she used to work. She decided to stop there and see what the firefighters knew. They told her all off-duty firefighters were being called in.

There was no time to waste. Berkman decided to join the firefighters from her old station. She did not have her gear with her, so she had to use whatever she could find. One firefighter loaned her a shirt. Someone else gave her a pair of shorts. The captain loaned her his turnout gear, which is the heavy coat and boots firefighters wear for protection. Other firefighters from the station had already taken the trucks. Berkman and the others borrowed a police van and began the drive to the World Trade Center site.

The Twin Towers of the World Trade Center had been the tallest buildings in New York City. Berkman expected that she and the others would be climbing the stairs to reach people. But the firefighters were shocked when they arrived. The Twin Towers were gone. "The towers had just fallen," Berkman said. "The air was like you were in a dust storm . . . but it was concrete and glass dust, everywhere." It was hard to breathe.

THE WORLD TRADE CENTER
The World Trade Center was made up of several office buildings around the Austin J. Tobin Plaza.

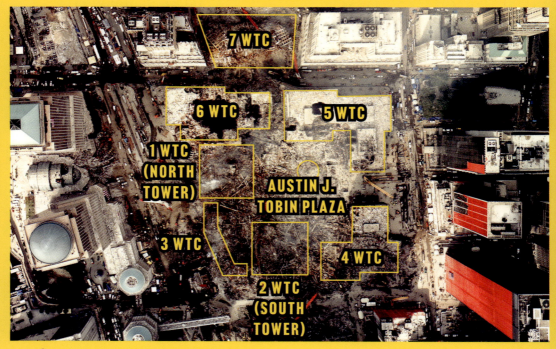

▲ The Twin Towers were each 110 stories tall. When they opened in 1973, they were the tallest buildings in the world.

The firefighters were scared. They could hardly see where they were going. The surrounding buildings were on fire. The ground was covered in **debris**. The situation was dangerous. But the firefighters knew they had to search for survivors in the other buildings, even if it meant putting their own lives at risk. Berkman was there when the 7 World Trade Center building collapsed. It was loud and terrifying. The ground shuddered like an earthquake. Berkman and the firefighters around her ran to avoid being caught in the falling debris.

Over the next few days, Berkman and other firefighters dug through piles of rubble more than 20 feet (6.1 m) high. They looked for survivors, working 12 hours or more each day. But before long, they realized they would not find many people who were still alive. That included other firefighters who were inside the towers when the buildings collapsed. Later, Berkman learned that 343 firefighters died on 9/11. She knew 250 of them. "We're just overwhelmed," Berkman said. "I just can't tell you how many of my close friends on the job are gone."

There were roughly 8,600 firefighters in New York City ►
on September 11, 2001. Nearly all of them were called to
respond to the attacks on the World Trade Center.

CHAPTER TWO

YAMEL MERINO

Yamel Merino was scheduled to work on the morning of September 11, 2001. She was an emergency medical technician (EMT). EMTs provide emergency medical care to people who are ill or injured but are not at a doctor's office or hospital. EMTs often help people who need medical care before they can reach a hospital. Sometimes those people are not injured badly. Other times, their lives are in danger. Merino and her EMT work partner would take people to the hospital in an ambulance. Every day was different.

That morning, Merino dropped off her son at her mother's house before she went to work. Merino worked in the **borough** of the Bronx in New York City. She had been an EMT for five years. Two years before, Merino's employer named her EMT of the year. Merino planned to become a nurse one day.

◀ **Yamel Merino's mother leans over Merino's coffin at a memorial service. Photos of Merino are visible on the left.**

Soon after Merino arrived at work on 9/11, she and her work partner learned that a plane had crashed into the North Tower of the World Trade Center. They hurried to their ambulance. People would need help from EMTs.

By the time they arrived at the World Trade Center, a second plane had struck the South Tower. Merino and her partner reported for duty near the South Tower. Everything was **chaotic**. People screamed and cried. They tried to run away from the World Trade Center. Many of them were bleeding. Merino and her partner tried to help as many people as they could. Some people were not badly hurt. But they did not understand what had happened or what they should do. Merino was still helping evacuees when the South Tower collapsed. She was buried in the rubble.

The next day, an EMT working with a specially trained dog discovered something in the debris of the South Tower. Crews gathered at the place where the dog smelled something. They hoped to find a survivor. But they found Merino's body instead. The crew carefully lifted her body out of the debris and put it on a stretcher. They covered her with an American flag. They realized they were not likely to find any survivors.

A New York City paramedic (left) and a police officer (right) breathe ▶
fresh oxygen near the World Trade Center on September 11, 2001.

Merino's boss broke the news to her parents. Just two months earlier, Merino had been at Disney World with her son. Now, she was gone. Merino's mother, Ana Jager, had once seen Merino rush to a burning car to pull children from the wreckage, even though it was her day off. Jager knew Merino would never turn away from people in need. Now her family would have to live on without her. "To lose a child, you don't wish that to your worst enemy," Jager said. "You'll never be the same."

In late 2001, the state of New York awarded Merino the EMT of the Year Award. She was also named one of *Glamour Magazine*'s Women of the Year that year. In 2005, Merino's son went to Washington, DC. He met President George W. Bush at the White House. President Bush awarded Merino the 9/11 Heroes Medal of **Valor**.

◄ **The space where the Twin Towers stood has been remade into 9/11 Memorial Plaza. The park includes the names of all 2,977 victims of the attacks in New York, Pennsylvania, and Washington, DC.**

CHAPTER THREE

WILLIAM JIMENO

William Jimeno was a rookie police officer. A rookie is someone who is just beginning his career. Jimeno worked for the Port Authority Police Department. The Port Authority works on transportation projects in New York and New Jersey. Such projects include building roads, airports, and tunnels.

◀ **Port Authority officers are responsible for looking after bridges, tunnels, ports, and airports.**

The Authority also owns the World Trade Center. The Port Authority Police Department works to keep travelers safe.

On the morning of September 11, 2001, the sun was shining and the sky was clear. Jimeno thought about taking the day off to go hunting. But he decided against it and made his way to work. He was assigned to a local bus station. While standing on the corner of 42nd Street and 8th Avenue, a huge shadow passed over him. "It completely covered the street for a split second," Jimeno said later. He did not know what it was.

Jimeno was called back to the Port Authority's office. There, he learned that American Airlines Flight 11 had struck the North Tower. He and the other Port Authority police officers were sent there to help rescue people in the building. Before he left, he called his wife to tell her what had happened and that he was OK.

Jimeno and several police officers hurried to a bus to travel to the North Tower. A second plane hit the South Tower while they were driving there. But Jimeno did not learn this until much later. When the officers arrived at the North Tower, they could hardly believe what they saw. There were wounded people everywhere. Sheets of paper filled the sky. They were coming from the windows that burst open in the explosion. Debris was falling.

Sergeant John McLoughlin asked for officers to go inside the North Tower to help fight the fires. Port Authority officers are trained to use firefighting equipment. Since Jimeno had graduated recently, his training was fresh. He volunteered. Jimeno also wanted to stick with McLoughlin. He knew that the sergeant had many years of experience. Jimeno thought he would be safest with him. A large underground area beneath the World Trade Center held a shopping mall, subway stations, and more. Jimeno and several others made their way underground. They were moving through a hallway between the North and South Towers when they heard a rumble. Jimeno later said, "Everything started shaking. I looked back toward the lobby, and I saw a fireball the size of my house coming."

Jimeno began to run toward a light that he hoped would take him outdoors. Suddenly, there was a rush of air like a strong wind. The hallway collapsed around the officers. Jimeno was hit by flying pieces of debris. Then everything was still. He found his radio and began calling for help. McLoughlin called the officers' names to find out where they were. Only two officers answered. The others had died.

They did not know it, but the officers were buried under 20 to 30 feet (6.1 to 9.1 m) of debris. Jimeno was trapped face-up. There were only inches of space between his face and the debris.

In the aftermath of 9/11, fires at the World ▶ Trade Center site burned for 100 days.

▲ John McLoughlin (left) and William Jimeno (right) pose with film director Oliver Stone at a screening of the film *World Trade Center* in 2006.

McLoughlin was curled up on his side, trapped about 15 feet (4.6 m) away. The third officer, Dominick Pezzulo, was able to get free. He tried to free Jimeno. But then the three men heard more rumbling. "It sounded like a humongous locomotive coming at us," Jimeno said. "All I could think was, *I'm gonna die*." Then the North Tower collapsed. More debris rained down on the officers. Pezzulo was badly injured and passed away. That left only McLoughlin and Jimeno.

The two men called for help and talked to each other. Each made sure the other stayed awake. Many hours later, people finally heard their calls for help. It took another three hours before rescuers could reach Jimeno and pull him out. McLoughlin was rescued several hours later. Both men had serious injuries and a long road ahead to recovery. But they were alive.

Jimeno has never forgotten that day and the terror of being trapped in the debris. He retired from the Port Authority Police Department in 2004. Now he talks to people, including students, about what happened to him on 9/11. He says, "As a survivor, I want everyone to know that there was more love than evil on that day. . . . As survivors, the way we honor all those that we lost is by being better human beings, keeping these memories alive, and talking about them."

CHAPTER FOUR

SCOTT STRAUSS AND PADDY McGEE

Scott Strauss was a New York City police officer who was part of the Emergency Service Unit (ESU). The ESU was a special unit with extra training. The ESU assisted police officers with emergencies. Strauss was taking a train home from work on September 11 when he learned that a plane had struck the World Trade Center. When he arrived at his home, he learned that a second plane had struck. He realized this could not be an accident. He grabbed some clothes and headed back to work.

Patrick ("Paddy") McGee was also an ESU officer. He was asleep at home that morning. His wife woke him up. She told him something was happening in the city. He went with her to watch the news. The newscaster thought a small plane had struck the World Trade Center. That did not make sense to McGee. He told his wife he was getting his uniform in case he needed to go in.

◄ Scott Strauss (left) had been working since 11:30 at night on September 10. By the time he was assigned to rescue victims of the attacks, he had been awake for nearly 20 hours.

Then they saw the second plane strike on live TV. McGee immediately got in his car and headed to work.

The streets were crowded with cars and people trying to get away. Ordinary people tried to direct traffic. The police who usually did this were all running to the World Trade Center.

Strauss and McGee met up at the police station. They got dressed and gathered rescue equipment. Then they got in a truck with other police officers and made their way to the World Trade Center. The North Tower had collapsed just before they arrived. The smoke was thick and black, making it almost impossible to see. The piles of debris were much taller than the officers. Steam rising from the debris meant that it was very hot. It would be dangerous to climb on or try to go through the debris. It was also likely to be unstable. That meant it could shift and move underneath them. If the debris shifted while they were on it, they could fall and be trapped, too.

Several hours went by. The officers could not find any survivors. Then they learned that two Port Authority officers had been discovered still alive. Those officers were William Jimeno and John McLoughlin. They were buried beneath 20 to 30 feet (6.1 to 9.1 m) of debris.

Strauss climbed up the pile of debris on steel beams. McGee was close behind. They learned that Jimeno and McLoughlin were trapped below them. Both Strauss and McGee jumped into a hole. There was not much space for them to move through the debris. They had to take off their safety equipment. That included their guns. They had never worked without this equipment before.

UNDER "THE PILE"

Rescue workers on 9/11 called the debris from the fallen towers "the pile." Jimeno and McLoughlin were buried under 20 to 30 feet (6.1 to 9.1 m) of debris.

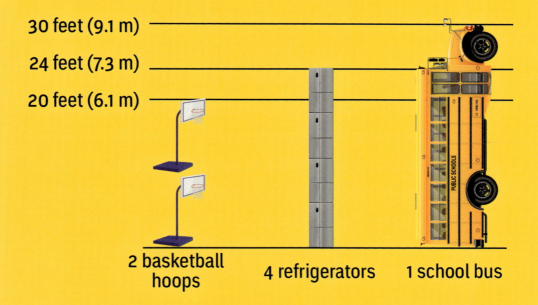

▲ **Smoke and dust covered New York City after the World Trade Center buildings collapsed.**

They used hand tools, knives, and even their bare hands to dig. At one point, they even used a pair of handcuffs. Other first responders formed a bucket brigade. A line of people passed buckets full of debris to people farther back in line. Those in the back emptied the buckets, then passed them up to fill again.

Three hours after they started, Strauss and McGee pulled Jimeno out of the debris and sent him to the hospital. Everyone was relieved. But Strauss and McGee did not realize that they had each been cut by debris. The hot steel burned through their clothes and shoes, all the way to their feet.

Strauss had to go to the hospital to get care for his injuries. McGee was still at the site. He knew McLoughlin was still trapped. But McGee was too exhausted to continue the difficult, dangerous work. He had cuts and needed oxygen to help him breathe, so he went to a nearby location where medics could help him. Other first responders went to work. It took several more hours before they could rescue McLoughlin.

Many people were inside the Twin Towers when they collapsed. Only about 20 of those people survived. Strauss and McGee helped save one of them. Jimeno and McLoughlin were some of the last survivors to be found in the World Trade Center rubble.

THINK ABOUT IT

- ▶ Why are first responders important in emergencies?
- ▶ Why is it important to have different types of first responders (such as EMTs, firefighters, and police officers) working at a disaster site?
- ▶ What do you think first responders do to help themselves be brave in scary situations?

GLOSSARY

borough (BURR-roh): A borough is a smaller part of a big city and has a government of its own. The Bronx is a borough of New York City.

chaotic (kay-AH-tik): Something chaotic is very confusing or disorganized. The World Trade Center was chaotic after the planes hit the towers.

debris (duh-BREE): Debris is made up of pieces of things that have been destroyed or broken down. Debris from the collapsed towers spread for blocks.

evacuated (eh-VAK-yoo-ayt-ed): People who are being evacuated are leaving a place where they might be in danger. Yamel Merino helped people being evacuated from the Twin Towers.

public transit (PUH-blik TRAN-zit): Public transit is the different types of transportation anyone can use to travel within a certain area, such as buses or subway trains. Public transit was stopped shortly after the September 11 attacks.

sergeant (SAR-junt): A sergeant is a police officer who is in charge of other officers. John McLoughlin was William Jimeno's sergeant.

terrorists (TAYR-ur-ists): Terrorists are people who commit violent acts to make people feel fear or terror. Terrorists flew airplanes into the Twin Towers on September 11, 2001.

valor (VAL-ur): Valor is bravery or strength in the face of danger. Yamel Merino was awarded the 9/11 Heroes Medal of Valor for her actions on September 11.

SELECTED BIBLIOGRAPHY

Strauss, Scott, and Eddie Reyes. "Retired NYPD Officers: We Dug Through the World Trade Center Rubble . . ." *Northwell Health*, 14 Sept. 2021, northwell.edu. Accessed 18 Oct. 2023.

Weinstein, Amy. "Emergency Medical Bag Tells Intertwined Story of Two Female First Responders." *9/11 Memorial Blog*, n.d., 911memorial.org. Accessed 18 Oct. 2023.

Willing, Linda. "Report from Ground Zero." *Women in the Fire Service, Inc.*, Sept. 2001, wfsi.org. Accessed 18 Oct. 2023.

FIND OUT MORE

BOOKS

Jimeno, William, and Charles Ricciardi. *Immigrant, American, Survivor.* New York, NY: Charles Ricciardi, 2021.

Rea, Amy. *Rescue Dogs on 9/11.* Parker, CO: The Child's World, 2025.

Romero, Libby. *September 11.* Washington, DC: National Geographic Kids, 2021.

WEBSITES

Visit our website for links about first responders on 9/11:
childsworld.com/links

Note to Parents, Caregivers, Teachers, and Librarians: We routinely verify our web links to make sure they are safe and active sites. So encourage your readers to check them out!

INDEX

Berkman, Brenda, 6–10
bucket brigades, 28
Bush, George W., 17

debris, 8–10, 14, 19, 20–23, 26–29

Emergency Service Unit (ESU), 25
EMTs, 13–17, 29

firefighters, 6–10, 20, 29

hospitals, 13, 28–29

injuries, 13, 14, 22–23, 28–29

Jager, Ana, 17
Jimeno, William, 18–23, 26–29

McGee, Paddy, 25–29
McLoughlin, John, 20–23, 26–29
Medal of Valor, 17
Merino, Yamel, 13–17

North Tower, 8, 14, 19–22, 26

Pezzulo, Dominick, 20–22
police officers, 18–29
Port Authority, 18–20, 23, 26
public transit, 7, 19, 25

7 World Trade Center, 8, 9
South Tower, 8, 14, 19–20
Strauss, Scott, 25–29
survivors, 9–10, 14, 23, 26, 29

working dogs, 14